POSSIBILITY

THINKING

THE ROAD MAP TO SUCCESS

BY

KINGSLEY C. STEWART

Table of Content

Introduction……………………………………..3

Chapter One

What is possibility thinking about?……………5

Chapter Two

Motivate Yourself To Succeed………………….13

Chapter Three

Success Comes With Peak Performance……….28

Chapter Four

The Power Behind Your Thought……………….49

Introduction

Possibility thinking is the bed rock to any success in life. Possibility thinking is a good developed philosophy for successful living. In order for one to be successful in this life he must develop "*it will work attitude*" towards all that he does.

Though success could have so many definitions by so many people, however this book has narrowed it down for you to understand the true meaning of success. There are two types of success; Deserved success and undeserved success. This book described the two in a way you would understand each of them and be able to follow through on how to obtain the better one.

In this book you will learn many things about success. Just to mention a few of what you are going to learn here are:

    i.   The motivation to succeed.

    ii.   The management skill to succeed.

    iii.   You will be inspired to catch a vision and achieve it.

    iv.   You'll be encouraged to try to succeed through your vision.

    v.   You'll become a possibility thinker and believe that nothing is impossible.

Success is to dare to dream the impossible dream, work on it with, expand every positive ideology and consistency, then seeing it come to reality.

To become successful through possibility thinking this book will teach you the four basic principles you must apply to become your own coach/mentor. They are, how to:

i. Identify and utilize your strengths & weaknesses.

ii. Identify the peculiarity of what motivates you.

iii. Discover what you need to hear and learn how to say it in such a way that you listen to your own advice and counsel.

iv. Determine what you can do to assure yourself to function at your best consistently.

CHAPTER ONE

What is possibility thinking about?

Possibility thinking is a good developed philosophy for successful living. In order for one to be successful in this life he must develop *"it will work attitude"* towards all that he does. Optimism is one of the best approaches in life to use in other to achieve success.

In fact, possibility thinking is a success system which works out wonders for those that practiced it. I have seen thousands of persons who have achieved incredible goals and overcome amazing obstacles and handicaps with the help of possibility thinking.

Success starts the day when you make up your mind and say to yourself *"I must be successful"*. Some people run from success with the ideology that success is evil or demonic. Some people believe that, for one to be successful he must soil his hands with devilish activities. They are embarrassed by the subject "*success*". After all, success has taken a lot criticism; most people see it as undeserved, while some see it as deserved.

Underserved success comes when success is achieved through exploitation of the poor, the weak, the oppressed; then such injustice is sinful. When people succeed in order to feed their insatiable greed, without caring of how people feel or what could be the resultant effect of their action on the people or the environment. This kind of success as aforementioned should be rebuked as it is not deserved.

Deserved success comes when it is not obtained through dubious means. However, the success obtained is equally used to improve the life of the people. The means through which this success is obtained is through things that would better the life of the people. This could be things like; research works and/or institutes, development of people oriented projects and establishment of businesses which does not have a negative effect on man-kind and its environment.

What does "*success*" means to you? Many people see this seven letter word from many angles. Let us see how many people had looked at success.

Success to some people means creating jobs to save the life of an entire town or nation. To others, it could mean a different thing all-to-gather, which could be accumulation of wealth. This could be ranging from buying land in all the states in the country to buying all the latest forms of manufactured cars or gadgets.

Success to some people is just obtaining winning position in any competition. In this, we must know that success is a process and not an end. It's more than what you read on the scorecard or scoreboard.

Success to some people is about setting goals and striving to reach them. Success is more than what you read in the final report or the published news release. Success in this case, should be accepting your God-giving opportunities and giving your divinely-inspired goals one hundred percent of your best effect without being pessimistic about them.

Some people see success as the ability to solve problems and resolve difficulties. This is true, but you must understand that success is a process that must not stop. If you must achieve success in problem solving, then you must proffer a solution which must be continuous to solving such a problem at any given time. If not, you have not achieved success in that field.

Some people see success as ability of acquiring fame and fortune. This is in no means a success. Fame and fortune are shallow goals unless they are a means to an end, a way to help others.

Success to some people means prosperity for the alternative to prosperity could be poverty. This is not the case of success as prosperity is the end but success is the process which is made continuous. How we look at success matters in life. It gives one the insight of how, when, where, and why he should be successful.

What is Success?

Success for the student means passing the courses in school and developing mind and talents to make a beneficial contribution to the human race. Success for the lawyer means helping confused persons extricate themselves from the tangled webs of conflicting involvements, setting them free again.

Success for teacher means motivating students to believe that they are smart – not seeing themselves as being stupid and helping students develop self-images that will lift them to heights they never before dreamed.

Success for the surgeon means continuous saving life through surgical operations.

Success for the husband and wife means making marriage work with the hope that they can celebrate a golden wedding anniversary. Success will mean keeping their family intact with communication lines open so this community of caring and sharing persons will enjoy each other in love.

Success for salesperson means discovering people

who have problems that will probably be solved by the sales-person's product(s) or service(s).

Success for the law enforcement officials and those in our military services means maintaining peace and order.

Success for the people who are ill means restored health or, at the very least, handling the illness in such a way that they inspire other around them.

Success can mean acquiring more money or material things. Surely our perception of success should not ignore the material needs of life. As Christians, we are not opposed to material success, if it means that people will be able to:

    i.   Provide for the development of their potential education.

    ii.   Enjoy health care.

iii. Start a business that could provide an outlet for their creative skills, the creation or distribution of a product or service and,

iv. Enable them to experience the "Joy of giving" to great movements, causes, ministries, and institutions in this world of hunger and pain.

Finally, success can be added up as having been proud of the person you have become by helping the people, community and environment to be where they are now and where they will be in future in terms of positive development.

More so, success is noblest when it leaves you with the self-respect that you have been a good steward of the life, liberties, possibilities and opportunities that God offered to you.

Success is to do something good, when you can,

where you can, while you can! If, down the road, a tragic collision "*ends it all about life*". It is not the case in the terms of success, nothing can ever really end it all. Success can progressively start with someone and continue generations after generations without ending.

Success is never ending because success is like the process of seed planting. Good seeds, honestly offered, immediately are transformed into fertile seeds. Every creative redemptive contribution, like a seed planted will bear fruit. Only God can count the apples in a seed. The farm can go broke or be sold to a developer, but the land won't evaporate. It will remain as a base of productivity for some one. Meanwhile, streams of human being were kept alive, for a season, by food from that farm. While those people were kept alive, they made love and bore children, and so the fruit of the seed goes on and on.

Possibility thinking will make you agree with me that, we owe our lives to successful people whom we'll never be able to meet personally to say "Thank You!".

- Consider the freedom we enjoy! Some soldiers died for that e.g fight against Boko Haram in Nigeria. His success goes on and on.
- Some medical researcher wiped out a disease years ago and in most cases at the expense of their own lives just to save generations of man-kind e.g the eradication of Polio and Ebola Virus from Africa and the ongoing Coronavirus of 2020.
- Some teachers helped to inculcate morals to our children and make them

continuously become responsible citizens from time to time.

These were just to mention but a few. In this vein, we all must be willing to help at all times in other to achieve success. A little good, helps a lot more than we will ever imagine, if that person who has been helped, will help somebody else. There is every need for you to know that the death of a caterpillar and birth of a butterfly do not mean that the caterpillar has stopped succeeding. This simply means that the continuation of caterpillar is in the birth of butterfly.

In this book you will learn many things about success. Just to mention a few of what you are going to learn here are:

vi. The motivation to succeed.

vii. The management skill to succeed.

viii. You will be inspired to catch a vision and achieve it.

ix. You'll be encouraged to try to succeed through your vision.

x. You'll become a possibility thinker and believe that nothing is impossible.

Success is to dare to dream the impossible dream, work on it with, expand every positive ideology and consistency, then seeing it come to reality.

It is fantastic to be successful as it is finding a need and filling it! Finding a hurt and healing it! Finding a problem and solving it! In this, we must remember that success cannot be achieved without a sacrifice.

To all who have made meaningful sacrifices to mankind, I say a big "Thank you!". Though they might not be alive today but their success is still duplicating continuously.

You too can be one of such people today!

The best time to embark on this journey is now!

CHAPTER TWO

2.0 Motivate Yourself To Succeed

If you were an Olympic athlete, enthusiastic audiences would cheer you on to great feats. If you were parts of a top sales team for a leading company, you'd attended regular seminars and training programs presented by experts who would charge you up and build your skills and confidence.

There's probably no greater power than the power to follow through on what you say you want to do. Whether it's being able to hit a tennis ball just where you want it to go, deliver a project on time within budget, or get yourself to deliver what you want to accomplish is truly a gift and an essential skill.

In fact, how often do we make promises to ourselves, set goals make New Year resolutions, or swear we'll do something- or never do something again- only to let ourselves down. According to a USA today report, nine out of ten Americans and even in other countries make New Year resolutions, but studies by Alan Marlatt from the University of Washington in Seattle shows that almost four out of five people fail to follow through their resolutions. If you must succeed in following through your resolutions, then you must be motivated and must remain on your motivation platform.

Furthermore, when you like what you're doing and you're committed to a clear purpose of course, following through on what you set out to do is less of a problem. Aren't we usually quite sincere making New Year's resolutions? So how do we know we'll be able to do better on our own? What about the days when you don't want to do what you know needs to be done? What about the things you don't like doing...the things you want to put off...the things you will get to later? All the best-made goals, schedules, routines, plans and to-do-lists are useless if you can't get yourself to turn them into action.

This is the same issue every professional athlete or performer must face. In every game, match, contest, show, they must ask themselves" will I be able to perform at my best upon demand?" To make sure they can, they have to train. They have to go through endless repetitions of moves or lines until they can do what it takes under the pressure of a competition or a production. This is essentially what is required of you to succeed. Though the athletes have coaches but on your own you are expected to succeed with little or no supervision.

Furthermore, you have to get to know yourself very well- so well that you know exactly what will get you motivated from time to time, what will calm you down and what will help you get focus; how to make sure you follow through on what needs to be done, when you'd rather not do it, how to keep yourself going when things take longer than you expected, and how to keep yourself going when you few like quitting or become impatient.

2.1 Four Steps to effective self-Management

To become a reliable mentor/coach for yourself, you must take four steps and these include:

v. Identify and utilize your strengths & weaknesses.

vi. Identify the peculiarity of what motivates you.

vii. Discover what you need to hear and learn how to say it in such a way that you listen to your own advice and counsel.

viii. Determine what you can do to assure yourself to function at your best consistently.

2.1.1 Identify and utilize your strengths and weaknesses

Often, your strength is measured in how you manage your weakness. We become successful with our own particular combination of experiences, talents, skills, resources, and assets. We also bring along our own personal limitations, concerns, doubts, and inexperience. Like any other coach, we've got to work with whatever strengths and weaknesses we bring to the game. To build our success, we've got to make the most use of what we've got including the good and not so good. However, every athlete, every racehorse, every actor and actress, every beauty pageant contestant or political candidate presents this very same challenge to their coaches and mentors.

In fact, one gymnast may excel on the balance beam but struggle with her vault; while another is so natural on vault but wobbly on the beam. One professional singer may sing like a master before a live audience but freeze in studio sessions, while another shies away from live performances but shines in the studio. One political candidate may be dynamic talking to the media and more reserved and distant at one-on-one fund raising, while another feels stiff and awkward appearing on television but is warm and engaging at in-person fund-raising. A volatile and stubborn but have amazing stamina and determination, while another may be cooperative and easygoing but tire easily and get sidetracked often.

Whatever the situation, at any given moment in time, the coach or trainer must strive to help those they manage make the most use of their strengths and work effectively around their weaknesses. And this helps you in managing your own independent career successfully. You need to have a realistic grasp of your strengths and weaknesses so you can make the most use of what you have to work with. In most cases, we are seen either over doing or under-doing what is required of us to be successful. So, thinking about it, when it comes to doing what's required to be successful, where do you shine? Where do you stumble? Where are you masterful? Where are you mediocre? What comes naturally to you? What do you struggle to achieve, without result?

These developed assessment tools are to help you take an honest look at the way things work out with you.

2.1.2 Assessing Your Ability To Perform Successfully:

In order to survive and thrive in any-thing you do, you must carry out six basic functions. For you to be successful, get going and stay afloat, you'll be called upon to carry out all six of these functions adequately and consistently whenever circumstances demand. While an organization recruit different individuals who shines at performing these different functions, when you're self-employed, you'll probably have to do them all yourself- at least in the beginning.

If you are like most people, when set out on your own, you're probably good or even masterful at some of these essential functions, but less good and even poor at others. Some things you can do with your eyes closed, while standing on one foot. Others may leave you cold, feeling inadequate, or wishing you could have root canal instead. As we describe these six functions and list the type of activities they involve, assess your strengths and weaknesses, preferences and natural proclivities. As you read through them:

i. Identify which of the six functions is the core function of your career circle that function (0).

ii. Under each function, check (v) the activities you do well and those that comes easily to you.

iii. Put an asterisk (*) alongside the activities you don't perform well at, dislike, or find difficult at doing.

1. **Creating:** In any operation, someone has to create the products and services that will be

provided to clients and customers. Of course, some independent careers are creative by nature. A sculptor, screenwriter, or novelist, for example, gets paid to create. It's their core function , but on one's own, not only must the artist do the other five functions, whatever your core function is, you too must be the creator, the visionary who conceives of what you'll be offering and how to make it appealing and valuable to those who need and will pay for it. So you'll be called upon to perform activities like these:

i. Imagining

ii. Designing

iii. Innovating

iv. Envisioning

v. Performing

vi. Perceiving

2. **Problem Solving:** In any venture, someone must figure out how to solve the inevitable problems involved in establishing an independent career like getting business, pleasing your clients and customers, and running your office effectively. Some independent careers- such as consultants, private investors, technical writers, information brokers, or software developers-are basically about problem solving. Solving problems is what they get paid to do. It's their core function, but whatever the core function of what you do is on your own, you too will need to engage at times in problem-solving activities such as:

   i. Analyzing
   ii. Diagnosing
   iii. Observing

iv. Investigating

v. Defining

vi. Evaluating

3. **Building:** Every independent career requires that someone roll-up his sleeves and do the hands-on work that gets and keeps things running. Some independent careers like construction, commercial cleaning services, swimming pool maintenance, computer repairs services, and hauling services gets paid to carry out such tasks. It's their core function. However, whatever your independent career is, from time to time, you too will have to engage in such activities as:

   i. Assembling

   ii. Computing

   iii. Repairing or Cleaning

   iv. Construction

v. Maintaining

vi. Transporting, Shipping and Packaging.

4. **Organizing:** Every operation needs someone to set up procedures, follow through, and carry out the day-to-day administrative task of operating as a business. People who have independent careers like professional organizers, indexers, medical claims processors, word-processors, or bookkeepers get paid to carry out such core functions. Getting and keeping things organized is their core function. Hence, on your own, whatever the core of your work, you too need to deal with the details involved in the financial clerical and legal aspects of your work. So, at times, you need to carry out such activities as:

i. Arranging

ii. Compiling and tracking

    iii. Gathering

    iv. Ordering

    v. Recording

    vi. Filling

5. **Leading:** In order to survive and thrive, any independent operation needs someone to oversee, coordinate, manage, market, sell, and promote its products and/or Services. In many careers like event planning, tour guide, public-relationship, specialist, manufacturer's rep and seminar leader, such activities are core function. So you'll need to engage in such activities as:

    i. Coordinating

    ii. Selling and promoting

    iii. Negotiating

    iv. Managing

    v. Marketing

vi. Influencing and persuading

6. **Improving:** In any operations, someone has to work personally with the customers and clients, listen to their needs, satisfy their complaints and identify where improvements need to be made. These kinds of interactions lead to the new and improved products and services that people coming back to you again and again people in some professions- like counseling, tutoring, errand services and message therapy- get paid to take care of and help people. That's their core function. However, whatever the primary nature of your work, you too must get sufficiently involved with serving your clients and customers to develop enough rapport and trust that they would want to continue doing business with

you. So, at times, you'll undoubtedly find yourself doing such things as:

i. Listening

ii. Caring

iii. Consulting

iv. Explaining

v. Teaching

vi. Helping

Chances are, for you to assess your performance and preferences for these six essential functions, you're fairly good at, if not masterful at your core function. If not, you'll need to sharpen your skills, so that people will believe in your abilities strong enough to want to pay you.

In order to survive and thrive, one of your key roles as your own mentor and coach will be to teach yourself how to start doing as good a job for yourself as you do for your clients.

2.1.3 Building On Your Core Function:

As long as you're reasonably good at and like doing your core function, it is your greatest strength and can serve as the foundation for your confidence and effectiveness. As your coach and mentor, you want to acknowledge, support, nurture, and encourage your proficiency at this function. Lead with it and then begin helping yourself build on this strength to get up to par at carrying out functions you don't like as much or do as well at. In this way, you can steadily expand the base of your competencies. It may mean seeking advice from outside experts and consultants, taking courses and seminars, learning from books, tapes, videos, and CD-ROMs, or when your budget allows it, hiring other people to help you carry out functions you dislike or do poorly.

What we've noticed is that, the most successful self-employed individuals rarely start being fully competent at all six of these key functions. In fact, over the years they become competent in them one by one. The artist who starts out petrified of selling finds ways to market himself comfortably. The highly technical software-developer turned consultant learns to listen to and communicate with customers who don't understand or want to know anything about computers.

As you've undoubtedly already discovered, not only do you usually have to carry out various aspects of these six functions, you must also learn to move quickly and easily from one of their essentials, but entirely different functions to another.

To be successful, it's your job to make sure you feel confident operating within your existing strengths and weaknesses while, at the same time, supporting and encouraging yourself to expand upon them so you'll become more of what you can be. And to do this, you must motivate yourself to do what need to be done, whether or not you like doing it, and whether or not you can do it as well as you'd like to do yet.

To succeed in life, you must learn to know how to use your strength to help others to improve their weakness. You must treat everybody fairly good enough.

2.2 Identifying What Motivates You

You must pay kin attention to notice and know whatever it is that motivates you to work. There is actually a wide variety of ways people motivate themselves. To some people, they feel motivated when they set up a reward for themselves for any deal or work completed or done successfully. However, some people get motivation from the satisfaction drawn from work completed. In this case, people thinks of the joy the work brings and they find it easy to do whatever is required to make sure they succeed. So people are motivated by amount of money they can make out of a deal or work. The money in view motives them to doing more and more of such thing. This is commonly found in a sales man's life.

Here are some other insights; self-employed individuals have had about how to motivate themselves:

i. When things look bad, I get discouraged and don't want to do anything much. So I've learned to tell myself the positive side of whatever's happening. I point out why it's not as bad as it looks and how it could even be better than I thought. Then, I feel like working all the harder.

ii. When some people are under the pressure of deadline, they get motivated in other to meet up with the deadline. But without the deadline, some people will have little or nothing done within a period of time. In this case, they will make the deadline look real so as to ask what will happen if they don't do this , and if it doesn't look good, then they would want to do it.

iii. However, some people think about the kind of person they want to be and if they are not living up to who they aspired to be like serves a real motivational tool for them. In this case, when the live up to expectation, then they feel happy that they did.

iv. Some people are motivated by facts and figures. They track their progress as if they are keeping a scorecard. In most cases, such people are motivated by their competitors as they would always want to stay at the top in whatever they do.

v. Knowing what de-motivates you is equally important. To some people revealing what they want to do to others is like writing the death sentence of such project. In such person, he prefers keeping the project secret until it has been started or completed before telling people. Here, telling people before the project are started de-motivates him. To begin identifying what motivates and/or de-motivates you;

i. Pay attention to what you complain about.

ii. What you get excited about,

iii. what gets you down and

iv. What picks you up.

Try always not to sell yourself short and let yourself get away with less than you know you can do, but make it as easy as possible for yourself to excel.

There are no wrong answers to these questions. The idea is to learn what you respond to. But you must learn not to use a negative comparism mechanism in assessing your performance. You must not compare yourself or get motivated by comparing yourself with only those you are better than.

Take your time and go through these questions and give your honest answers to them:

1. What is most important to you about what you are doing? What makes it what while? What makes it a drag?

2. How could you make doing something you need to do worth the effort? What would make you eager to get it done?

3. Which spurs you to do better: Compliments and positive feedback about what you've done well –or criticism of your performance and feedback on what you need to improve?

4. Are you more likely to strive to prevent negative things you fear might happen- happen-or to work toward attaining a positive outcome?

5. Do you thrive on competition? Does the opportunity to do better than someone else spur you on-or intimidate you?

6. Do you like to begin with the most pleasant tasks –or do you prefer to the worst over first and save the best for last?

7. Do you work better with the pressure of deadline-or do deadlines make you clutch?

8. Are you more interested in improving your own performance-or achieving more than someone else?

9. Do you work more efficiently when you wait until the last minute to meet your deadlines –or do you like to start early and finish ahead of time?

CHAPTER THREE

3.0 Success Comes With Peak Performance

To be really successful in anything you do, you have been motivated to make sure that you perform at the peak of your effort. However, peak performance helps you to remain at your motivated platform, and this as well enables you remain in business or services. In fact, you must know that "nothing good comes easy", "No gain without pain", "life operates on a give and take platform", etc. Like the computer terminology that says computer operates on garbage-in, garbage –out system. Likewise, success system operates in the same manner.

For you to be successful, you must make effort/input. This, notwithstanding should be coupled with peak performance. Peak performance requires you to be consistent, up and doing, patient and having a good motivational attitude to what you do at every given time.

3.1 What To Do When You Don't Feel Like Doing What Needs To Be Done

What do you do with yourself when you know what you need to do, but you don't want to do it? At one time or another, we're all faced a rapidly approaching deadline only to discover ourselves doing everything under the sun to achieve the set up goal. As you've probably already found at times, like this, begging, pleading, blaming and shaming do not work, but you must do the work. In most cases, trying to force yourself to do it doesn't work either. Now you want to be on your own, you know you can do whatever you want, even if it doesn't seem as though you can. So when you don't feel like doing what needs to be done, then you must have to find a way to get yourself to do it willingly.

In other words, you need to find out what would make doing the task at hand sufficiently desirable for you to get actively involved in getting it done. That means, you have to believe that it's worthwhile, possible, and intriguing enough to activate your participation. Here are several avenues to consider:

1. Ask yourself, what you want to do now. Sometimes you're perfectly willing to carry out a particular task at a later time; you just don't want to do it now.

2. Ask yourself, when you would be willing to do it.
3. Ask yourself, if you still want it to be done. If not, why not? Does it really need to be done?
4. Ask yourself, if you're willing to live with the consequences of not doing it.
5. Ask yourself, what you would be willing to do. Sometimes, there is part of what needs doing that you are willing to do and once you get started you may find that's all it takes to get you going.
6. Ask yourself, how else it could get done. You may find yourself having plenty of energy and interest, for example, in arranging for someone else to do it.
7. Ask yourself, how you will feel once you have done it. Sometimes, the prospect of having done it will activate you.

8. Ask yourself, why you don't want to do it some time, you can alter aspects of what needs to be done to make it more appealing.
9. Ask yourself, how long you would be willing to do just a little at a time.
10. Ask yourself, what would make you want to do it.

Here's a formula for how to get you going from psychologist Stanley coren of the University of British Columbia.

Most Important+Easiest+Quickest=Best Place to Start

Make a list of what you want to accomplish during a particular work period. Identify which steps are the most important and which you can do the most quickly and easiest start with the most important steps you can do most quickly and easily.

3.2 Strategies for effective peak performance

Preparing yourself to work at your peak is much easier when you're on your own, particularly, if you're on your own at work and greater control over the course of your day, making this, there are five-basic steps we're going to pass through in other to get an effective peak performance.

Step 1: Remain Relaxed Under Pressure

Often times you notice yourself to be hot but sometimes you're not. We all have times when we drag through the day, times when nothing seems to go on right. Obviously, we can't be hot all the time. The trick is to be hot when you need to be.

When you need to be at your best, when you need to perform at your peak, you want to feel relaxed and confident. You want to be calm, alert, and in charge. Unfortunately, it's too often true that the more important the moment, the higher the pressure and the less relaxed and composed we feel. At key moments, instead of enjoying a state of relaxed confidence, you may feel your heart racing and your palms sweating. Your brain may feel as if it's either stuck in slow motion or on fast-forward.

This experience is commonly seen, after all, we are usually doing things that are new to us. We may not even know that someone, somewhere have done a similar thing before. There is every need for us to know how to turn this fear and anxiety into confidence. Here are few quick and easy techniques that are useful to get and stay relaxed at any time throughout the day.

1. **Learn to notice quickly when your body is beginning to feel tense:** Notice when in your body you feel tense, tight, hyper, creepy, queasy, and shaky. Then take action to return to a relaxed state immediately, before the tension builds ups.

2. **Take several long, deep breaths:** Slow, deep breathing sends a signal to the brain that accompanies a relaxed state. So anytime your day gets harried and you start to feel uptight, take a few slow, deep breaths. Count from 1 to 10 as you inhale

and from 10 to 1 as you exhale. Take five to ten of these relaxing breaths until your breathing becomes calm and rhythmic.

3. **Shake out the tension:** Take a moment to shake out the areas of your body that begin to feel tense and tight. Shake out your hands, arms, head, feet, legs, and finally your whole body. Do these until you feel some relief.

4. **Take a break in a relaxing local Area:** Research shows that being in a natural setting can reduce stress. Even viewing scenes of nature reduces muscle tension, blood pressure and heart rate in individuals under pressure and help them recover from stressful events, including surgery, etc more quickly.

However, the environmental psychologist Stephen Kaplan found that you can benefit from the stress-reducing advantages of nature simply by spending a few moments looking out the window or walking through a garden. Watching sunrises and sunsets is particularly relaxing. If you don't mind getting wet, standing in the rain is an unusually renewing experience so when you feel uptight, go outside.

- Lie under a tree on the grass.
- Sit in the breeze on the porch.
- Walk in the park, or if you have water nearby, stroll by the river, lake, or ocean.

Of course, outdoors is not the only place you can relax. Many people take solace from visiting a museum, art gallery, Spa, or public monument. You can even create a special room or area of your home for relaxation, quiet reflection and/or meditation. You might even want to decorate and design your entire home to have a calming and restorative quality.

5. **Take a mental mini-vacation:** If you can't get away even for a few minutes, close your eyes and imagine that you are in one of your favorite natural environments or some other relaxing place, the sun set over the ocean, sitting by a bubbling brook in the mountains, or curled up in your favorite book.

6. **Play relaxing background music:** Recently, research have shown that human brain and body are highly sensitive to sound, and especially music. Certain types

of music have a particular rhythm and cadence that has been found to induce a calm, relaxed state of mind even when played softly in the background.

7. **Eat the right food:** Good nutrition can help you stay relaxed, too. Research has shown that you eating some foods pick you up while some relaxes you. The book "Managing your mind and mood through food" by Judith Wurtman a researcher at the Massachusetts institute of Technology, recommends that to feel more relaxed, you should eat complex carbohydrates like breads, muffins, pasta, cereals, potatoes, and grains. Research shows that B-Vitamin is good for stress management while C-Vitamin is good for stress reduction. B-Vitamins are seen in grains and leafy green

vegetables while C-Vitamins are seen in green peppers, strawberries, salmon, etc.

8. **Use your natural alarm clock:** Normally, the sound of an alarm clock starts your day in distress. It jangles you awake and puts your system into panic. When you go to bed early enough, all you need to do is take a deep breath counting from 10 to 1. Then, mention the actual time you would want to walk up. Do this up to ten times like: "I will walk by 5:00 AM, I will walk by 5:00 AM, ..." When you have done this, as a beginner keep a watch near you so that when you wake, you can confirm it. In most cases, you will find out that you will wake few minutes before the set time. Natural clock usage will go a long way in helping you to control and manage stress.

9. **Enjoy a pet Break:** Stroking and playing with a pet can help reduce stress and even extend life. Petting an animal actually reduces blood pressure, as does watching fish swim around in an aquarium.

10. **Daily Meditation:** A large body of scientific researchers now shows that daily meditation is one of the best, most reliable ways to condition your mind to function in a perpetually calm and relaxed state. Research shows that meditating regularly lowers levels of stress hormones and plasma cortisol, both of which go up with stress, and reduces cardiovascular risk. As a result, it can improve your mood, reduce stress, lower your blood pressure and cholesterol level improve your sleep, slow the aging process, increase your

productivity, and speed up the rate at which you learn. And all it takes is twenty minutes a day!

STEP 2: Get Energized! Stay Energized!

Fatigue is the number one symptoms people complain about to their doctors yet the most successful people seem to have boundless energy. They always seem ready to take on any challenge. They jump out of bed raring to go and they're still going full steam ahead come evening. How do they do it? Here are several ways to get charged up and stay that way.

1. **Get plenty of Relaxation:** Sometimes, people question why we put so much emphasis on making sure you don't over

work. Perhaps it's because we both tend to be over workers. But more than that it's because we know that you can't be at your best when you're tired, worn out, and dragging. It's like overtraining. If you overtrain before a competition or performance, you're burned out when the actual event arrives.

More so, it's an illusion to think you'll get further by overworking. When you're overworked, you don't think at your best, or make the best decisions. In other to remain energized, you must access yourself from time to time to know the level of work load you can carry as a person.

2. Keep the Pressure in bounds:

Unrealistic expectations are the real culprit in burnout. Burnout occurs when the demands we put on ourselves out-weigh our energy supply. On the job, we might blame overly demanding bosses for the burnout we experience. But on your own, it's your own unrealistic demands that slow you down and sabotage your performance.

In fact, high expectations are a good way to motivate ourselves to go beyond unnecessary limits. Nevertheless, success requires a delicate balance between the energy we have available and the demands we place on ourselves. When energy and demand are equal, we perform at our peak. If we don't believe, we tend to make unreasonable demands on ourselves in order to compensate, and ultimately our performance suffers. On the other hand, when we believe fully in our ultimate success, we instill in ourselves the confidence to work at a sensible pace, and our performance improves. Don't allow people, friends and/or family pressurized you into what you know you can't handle at any particular time.

3. **Know how much sleep you need and make sure you get enough:** The researchers' shows that most people get 20 percent less sleep today than we did 100 years ago. Evidently, when there are no enough hours in the day to finish our planned work, we take them from the night. But, don't shortchange yourself for more than one or two nights in a row. For some people, eight hours of sleep is a must; for others slightly less or slightly more is required. The goal is to get enough sleep

each night that you raise feeling refreshed, but not so much that you feel sluggish. You can find your peak level by noticing how you feel in the morning. Schedule your most demanding work for those times of day when you are at your peak. Leave less arduous tasks like sorting mail and filing for low energy period.

4. **Insist at taking at least one day-off every week:** You need this break to relax and recharge. Taking off two days a week is even better. If for certain short periods you can't squeeze out a day off every week, insist on at least a day a month.

5. **Make Sure You are Enjoying What You Do:** There's Nothing like loving what you do to boost your energy and keep you going. Usually, when you first go out on your own,

you're excited and turned on by what you're doing, but sometimes after doing it day after day, you don't like it as much as you thought you would. Or after a while, you may feel the need to go on to other things. When this happens, if you force yourself to continue doing what you've been doing, you'll start dreading "Monday again!" You'll begin dragging through the day, going through the motions, and slacking off. So watch for signs that your creative energies are warning and allow yourself to find ways for your business to evolve with you. In most cases, doing a perfect work will continually energize and refresh you.

6. **Eat high-energy Foods:** Research shows that a person can manage his mind and mood through food. High energy food

increases mental alertness, and greater motivation. This can be obtained by eating; protein-rich foods like fish, Chicken, and lean beef, low-fat dairy products, dried peas and beans, grains, seeds and nuts. You should leave out or minimize energy drainers like alcohol, sugar, salt, coffee, and junk food, which seem to charge you up but actually stress you out. Keep healthy, high-energy snacks on hand like pumpkin seeds, almonds, carrots, hard-boiled egg, grapes and whole-grains bread.

7. **Get Plenty of Exercise:** Do an aerobic exercise (swimming, Running, cycling, Dancing) at least twenty to thirty minutes every single day. Choose an activity you enjoy. Being on your own, especially if your work at home allows you more options for

fitting exercise into a busy day. You can notice and choose the time that works out best for you to exercise, but it is better in the morning or latter in the evening.

8. **Take Vacations:** At least once a year, take off a week or more to truly get away from your work and your regular routines and responsibilities. Often self-employed individuals feel that they don't have the time or money for a vacation. In fact, extended break period provides fresh energy new perspectives and renewed clarity for your business. You can tag a holiday at the end of a business trip to help you reduce cost.

STEP 3: Build Your Concentration

Concentration in this contest is the ability to focus all your energy on accomplishing the task at hand. In competitions, peak performers develop the ability to focus, to concentrate on their goals no matter what's going on around them. How do they respond reality to any event that's pertinent to the task at hand and ignore all else? Here's what we've observed.

They know exactly what they want to do and what it takes to do it. They aren't asking themselves, "Do I really want to get that shot in now or should I wait until later? They aren't wondering "should I put the ball in this hoop or some other one? "They know what they need to do.

They turn the performance over to the moment. The preparation, practice, study, strategy and so on are behind them, and they give 100 percent of their energy and attention to what is going on second by second, short by shot, stroke by stroke. They are not interested in their past nor future but that present time to achieve their goal.

We can each develop this ability to concentrate totally, but it requires a commitment and a willingness to set up our lives so that we can devote our full attention to the tasks at hand for example, you can do any or all of the following:

1. **Make adequate child-care arrangements:** So you wouldn't be distracted by family and other parental

responsibilities. Some people mistakenly think they can work with children underfoot but that does not help your business as you can't have 100 percent concentration on your work.

2. **Set up time signals:** This will help you not to continually watch the clock. You can use a digital watch to alert you when it's time to move on to other activities. You Can Set up time to enable you know when session of an activity should end.

3. **Use an answering machine or answering services:** This will help you to work without any phone call interruption. When you need to focus on key tasks, set aside a time of day to return phone calls instead of taking or making them at random.

4. **Take definite action:** Once you get set on a course of action or act. Then evaluate, commit to a course of action and observe the results. Don't over analyze plans before swinging into action.

5. **Get the cooperation of family and friends:** You should make your family members and your friends know your work concentration time so that they will not distract you in such time.

6. **Locate your office or work space away from disruptions and distractions:** Attics, garages, back rooms, and rooms off the garage make ideal home offices. Offices at the ends of corridors or set off from customer areas

can help you concentrate more effectively in your work place.

STEP 4: Become an Optimist

Nothing splendid has ever been achieved except by those who dared believe that something inside them was superior to circumstance. Worry is one of the biggest drains on our energy. It saps enthusiasm and confidence faster than any other activity. More so, misuse of our imagination is regarded as worry. Instead of using the imagination to project positive outcomes, the worrier imagines dreaded disasters and defeats. Optimists, on the other hand, use their imagination to rehearse success.

Indeed, we find out that the most successful individuals from all walks of life do this routinely. Meanwhile, not only do optimists imagine a rosy future, they remember their successes much better than they recall their failures. They also dwell on the pleasant world. They skip over, although they don't ignore, their shortcomings but they rely more on their achieved success.

Research is now confirming that optimists are more successful in all areas of life. Recent studies shows that optimists excel in school, have a better health and may even live longer. Optimists `also do better in the face of stress. They take action sooner, break big problems into small, more manageable units; Stick to their goals longer, and believe others can help. Optimists also report less fatigue, depression, dizziness, muscle soreness, and coughs than pessimists when facing the same stressful events.

If you tend to be pessimistic by nature, here are a few things you can do to make optimism a regular habit.

1. **Stop hoping and start anticipating:** Think for a moment of something that you want very much to come true. Most people feel much better anticipating the results they want. Hoping usually involves imagining two outcomes: the one you want and the one you don't want. It's usually accompanied by an uneasy sense of yearning. Anticipation, on the other hand, usually involves thinking of only one result: the one you want.

More often than not, it's accompanied by a sense of excited expectation.

2. **If you must worry, do it on a schedule:** The Pennsylvania state University Psychologists Thomas Borkovec and Elwood Robinson Suggest that chronic worrywarts contain their worry by setting aside thirty minutes a day in which they can worry. All worry is to be saved for this one period, during which they can worry as much as they please.

3. **Associate with Optimists:** Optimism is contagious, so cultivate positive, upbeat friends and acquaintances. Avoid spending time with naysayers, complainers and doomsayers. Join upbeat

organizations and groups; avoid downbeat ones.

4. **Listen to upbeat songs:** Have you ever noticed that popular vocal music generates intense feelings- usually sad, wistful, Lustful, or romantic one? What if you were to put this same emotive power of music to work to generate joyful, optimistic, empowering, stimulating, and exciting feelings? You should look out for inspiring and empowering songs and make them your daily interest.

STEP 5: Be There Now

When completely focused on the present, logical and analytical processes are suspended and as this occurs, the peak performer has the sense that all actions are occurring automatically and effortlessly. Have you ever missed an opportunity because you didn't see it coming? If so, chances are you were distracted, lost in thought, living in your own world, listening to yourself talk or day-dreaming when the vital clues of great things passed you by. In fact, daydreaming is a great way to relax and get away from it all. But when the situation calls for you to be on your toes, you need to be fully present in touch with what's going on around you and be able to respond quickly and appropriately.

Furthermore, to succeed in life, you must be very sensitive to all that happens around you. You must always be willing and able to provide solution to people's problem. Your senses must be turned to hear, see and sense everything around you. In the field of neuroliquistics programming, this state of awareness is referred to as being in up time.

The key to successfully focusing on the present is learning to be attentive to your senses and to the quality of what you are sensing, rather than to focus on your interpretation of the meaning. So, the first way to begin with your skills of awareness is to operate more often in up-time and become more aware of what you are and are not aware of. Here are a few simple exercises that you can use to heighten your sensory awareness.

1. **Become an Observer of your Awareness:** Take a moment to observe where you have your attention. Say to yourself, "*I am aware of ...*" and finish the sentence with whatever you become aware of at the moment. You'll notice how quickly your attention moves. As it does identify whether what you are aware of is:

    i. **An inner sensation:** A pain, an itch, a feeling, an emotion, tightness, fullness, a hunger, a thirst. Peak performers quickly calibrate feedback from inner sensations.

ii. **An outside Stimulus:** An object or event you see, touch, taste, smell, or hear. Peak performers block out superfluous stimuli and are hyper-alert to relevant ones.

iii. **Mental activity:** Thoughts, explanations, interpretations, guesses, comparisons, plans, remembered events or activities, daydreams. Mental activity is downtime. It takes you into your head and way from your present experience. Thought stops romance.

2. Focus On Each Area of Awareness: Begin by noticing your inner sensations. Notice if your body is relaxed. Where does your body feel tight? How do you feel right now? Mad? Sad? Glad? Scared? Excited? Bored? Agitated? Peaceful? How do your toes feel? Your stomach; Shoulders, fingers, elbows, earlobe?

Now with your score-card, shift your attention to outside sensations. Look around the room, what do you notice? What do you hear? Do you suddenly become aware of sounds you didn't hear before? The clock ticking? Can you smell anything? Now move about and tough things around you. Notice the sensations- soft, smooth, hard, sharp, rough, cold, and hot.

As you do this, notice if you begin evaluating or thinking about these things or if you just let yourself experience them. This aspect will always help you to get focused in anything you want to achieve with little or no distraction or abstract mind.

3.3 Making Success Automatic

The suggestions made earlier in this chapter will enable you access a peak-performance state wherever you need to. When you need to perform optimally, you'll be able to move into this highly productive state. Over time, when the pressure is on, when the stakes are highly you'll automatically relax, feel energized, focus, anticipate doing your best, and remain in the moment. If your heart starts racing or your energy starts lagging, you will automatically say and do the right thing to slow yourself down or charge yourself up. Conditioning yourself for peak performance is like setting the automatic thermostat on your heating and air-conditioning system, it notifies itself to kick in. Once, the optimal level is reached, however, it cuts back. However, it is with learning how to keep yourself in a state at which you can perform optimally that will help you to function automatic.

As your own coach and manager, you can train yourself to achieve a superior result any time. Its matter of making sure you can count on yourself to do what you want to do and what you tell yourself and others that you will do. It's a matter of knowing what motivates you and how to tap that motivation when you need it, and then being in peak mental, physical and emotional condition.

CHAPTER FOUR

4.0 The Power Behind Your Thought

4.1 Your Thought Shows In Your Character

Sometimes people think that they behave in a different way from the way they think, but the simple answer to this is "No" Your character is a radiation of your thought.

In fact, the book of proverbs 23:7 proclaims, *"For as he (a man) thinketh in his heart, so is he"* This adage reaches out to every condition and circumstance of human endeavor. Each of us is literally what we think, our character being the complete sum of all our thoughts.

More so, thoughts and character are like seeds and plants. There could hardly be a plant without a seed. Plants spring out from seeds and bear fruits that in-house the seed. This could be direct or indirect seeds. In fact, as seed is to plant, so is thought to character. The outward manifestation of what we think is what shows up in our character. In this, every one of our acts springs from the hidden seeds of thought and could not have appeared without them.

It is very important for you to know that action is the blossom of thought, while joy and suffering are its fruits; thus do we dwell in the sweet and bitter harvest of our own planning. We all are shaped, framed, molded and formed by the way and manner we think. If your mind is filled with evil thoughts, then you will definitely ripe pain and suffering, but if your mind is filled with good thoughts, then you will ripe joy and happiness as your fruit of labor.

The way we think obviously affects our growth. However, growth in human life is a natural phenomenon and not a creation by artifice. Cause and effect is as absolute and undeviating in the hidden realm of thoughts as in the world of visible and material things. A noble and God-like character is not a thing of favor or chance but is natural result of continuous effort and right thinking, the effect of long-cherished associated with God-like thought. An ignoble and bestial character, by the same process is the result of the continued harboring of groveling thoughts.

The fact still remains that, we are the product of our thoughts and actions (character). In this case, we are either made or destroyed by ourselves through our thoughts and actions. Our thoughts and actions have long served as equipment used to fashion the weapons by which we are destroyed. At the same time, the same thought and character have served as laudable equipment which helps people to build heavenly mansions of joy, strength and peace.

The right choice of thought and character puts us in the right state of true human status-quo but the wrong choice of thought and character puts us in the false state of human status-quo other-wise known as the behavioral level of the beast. The two extreme states in human life are the "*perfection state* (True human state)" and the "*Beast State* (false human State)" These two extreme human states are obtainable to any man otherwise, it is a matter of choice. You can choose on the side you will belong.

As the lord of our own thoughts which controls our power, intelligence, and Love, each of us holds the key to every situation and contains within ourselves that transforming and regenerative agency by which we may make ourselves what we will.

Though each of us is always our own master, even in our weakest and most abandoned state in life. Nevertheless, in a state of weakness and degradation of life, we become foolish masters and misgovern beings. When we begin to reflect upon our condition and to search diligently for the law upon which our being is established, we then will become wise masters, directing our energies with intelligence and fashioning our thoughts to fruitful issues. Such is the conscious master, and we can only thus become by discovering is totally a matter of application, self-analysis, and experience.

Nothing good comes easy by such searching and mining are gold, diamonds obtained. We can find every truth connected with our being, if we will dig deep into the mine of our soul; and that we are the maker of our own character, the molder of our own destiny. If we will watch, control and alter our thoughts by linking cause and effort through patient practice and investigation, we will obtain that knowledge of ourselves which is understanding, wisdom and power. In other for any man to enter the door of the temple of knowledge, he must patiently practice and have ceaseless importunity to what he seeks.

4.2 Effect of Thought on Opportunities and Circumstances:

Like a garden which can be cultivated and/or maintained or allowed to run wild, so is the human mind. Garden, whether cultivated or not, the grasses must grow. It could either be called weeds when not cultivated or crops when cultivated. In the case of human being, nurtured mind when it meets with opportunity, it produces positive result. But, if the mind is not nurtured, when it meets with opportunity, it produces a bad result.

Nevertheless, to obtain a good result, one must continuously pursue the process of weeding his thought off all the wrong, useless and impure thoughts. One must equally learn, the new way through which he can cultivate towards perfection, the fruits and flowers of right, useful and pure thoughts in order to maximize opportunities.

The philosophy built around the thought-forces and mind elements operates in the shaping of our character, circumstances, and destiny. This process reveals within ourselves the laws of thought and enables us to understand with increasing accuracy how our thoughts and mind functions.

Thoughts and character are two elements in one container. As character can manifest and discover itself only through environment and circumstance. The outer conditions of our life will always be found to be harmoniously related to our inner state. In fact, circumstances at any time does not wholly reflect our full character but it shows that those circumstances are so intimately connected with some vital thoughts-element within ourselves that for the time being, they are indispensable to our development.

Where you are now is the product of your being. The thoughts which you have built into your character have brought you here now. In the arrangement of life, there were no room for empty space or chance, but all were a result of a law which cannot err. As aforementioned like the garden is the mind. You must cultivate the culture of progressive inclination in positive thinking.

As progressive and evolving being, you are where you are today that you may learn and grow. You have been buffeted by circumstances so long as you now believe yourself to be the creature of outside conditions; but when you realize that you are a creative power and that you have the hidden soil and seeds of your life to germinate and grow out from the circumstance, you then become the rightful masters of yourself.

Meanwhile, circumstances grow out of thought, for you know that, whoever has for any length of time practiced self-control and self-purification, knows- for we will have noticed that the alteration in our circumstance has been in exact ration with our altered mental condition. The truth is that, when we earnestly apply ourselves to remedy the defects in our character and make swift, we progressively pass rapidly through a succession of vicissitudes.

Just as implied in the case of the garden, where there is no free space, so is the mind. The human mind must be filled with content of elements of thought at all times. This could be thoughts of either good or evil or mixed at any given time. Therefore, every thought-seed sown or allowed to fall into the mind and to take root there must germinate, grow and produce its own. It will certainly blossom sooner or later into action and bearing its own harvest of opportunity and circumstance. It is obvious and true that good thoughts bear goo fruits while bad thoughts bear bad fruits.

Following the inmost desires, aspirations, thoughts by which we allow ourselves to be dominated (Pursuing the frivolities of impure imaginings or steadfastly walking the highway of strong and high endeavor), we at last arrive at their fruition and fulfillment in the outer conditions of our lives. The laws of growth and adjustment are naturally followed in all our endeavor.

Furthermore, it is important for you to know that, one does not come to drunkenness or crime by the tyranny of fate or circumstance but by the pathway of groveling thoughts and base desires. Neither does a pure-minded person fall suddenly into crime by stress of any mere external force; the criminal thought, had long been secretly fostered in the heart, and the hour of opportunity revealed its gathered power of germination and growth. No such conditions can exist as descending into vice and its attendant suffering apart from vicious inclinations, or ascending into virtue and its pure happiness without the continued cultivation of virtuous aspirations. Therefore, as the lord and master of our thoughts, we are the makers of ourselves, the shaper and author of our environment. Even at birth, researchers says that, the soul comes to its own, and through every step of its earthly pilgrimage, it attracts those combinations of conditions which reveal itself, which are the reflections of its own purity and impurity, its strength and weakness.

However, we do not attract that which we want but that which we are freely drawn to us naturally. Our whims, fancies, and ambitions are thwarted at every step, but our inmost thoughts and desires are fed with our own food, be it foul or clean. The "divinity that shapes our ends" is in us: Thought and action are the jailers of fate- they imprison, being base; they are also the angels of freedom- they liberate, being noble. Not what we justly earn directly or indirectly. The truth remains that our wishes and prayers are gratified and answered only when they harmonize with our thoughts and actions. In this vein, you cannot be the same time refuse to work then your prayers will definitely remain un-answered.

All of us are anxious to improve our circumstances, but are unwilling to improve ourselves. We therefore remain bound as people who do not shrink from self-crucifixion and can never fail to accomplish the objective upon which our heart is set. In most cases, we do things wrong (unconsciously) while perhaps arming at a good end, therefore continually frustrating our accomplishment by encouraging thoughts and desire which cannot possibly harmonize with our desired end result.

Suffering is always the effect of wrong thought in some direction. It is a pure indication that one is out of harmony with himself and laws of life. Suffering is the element of purification (i.e like fire to Gold) to the sole of man. Therefore, the circumstance we encounter with suffering are the result of our own lack of mental harmony. When our being (i.e spirit, soul and body) is in a grate harmony, we enjoy the state of purity and this makes us to work stress less.

When you accept suffering as path of life that must be followed to obtain purity. Then, you adapt your mind to the regulating factor: which cease to name others as the cause of your conditions but begin to build yourself up in strong and noble thoughts; which cease to kick against circumstances but begin to use them as aids to more rapid progress and as a means of discovering the hidden powers and possibilities within you.

When you radically alter your thoughts, you will be astonished at the rapid transformation it will affect the material condition of your life. You may imagine that thought could be kept secret, but it cannot; it rapidly crystallized into habit, and habit solidifies into circumstance. In order to drive home this idea; lazy thoughts crystallize into habits of unseemliness and dishonesty, which solidify into circumstances of foulness and beggary;

Thoughts of fear, doubt, and indecision crystallize into weak, soft and irresolute habits, which solidify into circumstances of failure, indigence and slavish dependence and thoughts of courage, self-reliance and decision crystallize into habits of cleanliness and industry which solidify into circumstances of pleasantness.

If we will watch, control and alter our thoughts, by linking cause and effort, through patient practice and investigation we will obtain that knowledge of ourselves which understands, wisdom and power.

www.ingramcontent.com/pod-product-compliance
Lightning Source LLC
Chambersburg PA
CBHW050244220526
45465CB00002B/548